ROTARY SNOWPLOWS
ON THE
CUMBRES & TOLTEC SCENIC RAILROAD

Joseph P. Hereford, Jr.

with an article by Earl G. Knoob

WINDY POINT
P R E S S

Book design: Steven Schroeder, Albuquerque, NM

Printing: Cottonwood Printing Company, Inc., Albuquerque, NM
Imagesetting: Business Graphics, Inc., Albuquerque, NM
Internegatives: Kerry Nelson, Image Masters, Albuquerque, NM

Library of Congress Catalog Card Number: 94-61917
ISBN 0-9644399-0-5

COVER: Rotary snowplow OY of the Cumbres & Toltec Scenic Railroad clearing about two feet of snow from the track, May 25, 1983. The plow train is working east from Cumbres, Colorado, approaching mile-post 329.

TITLE PAGE: Cumbres & Toltec Scenic Railroad rotary snowplow OM plowing about two miles north of Chama, New Mexico, on February 15, 1976. The event was one of four Winter Specials operated on the C&TS in the 1970s. Photograph by Clif Palmer.

ACKNOWLEDGMENTS

The author wishes to express his appreciation to the numerous individuals whose assistance made this effort possible. Darrell T. Arndt, James P. Bell, Roger Breeding, John Chenowith, Tom Klinger, Earl G. Knoob, George Lawrence, William J. Lock, William Moyers, Jr., Clif Palmer, Ernest W. Robart, and Richard Sons generously made available their photographs of the C&TS rotary snowplow operations.

Thanks also to Roger Breeding, W. George Cook, Peter Gilbert, Tracy Guidry, Earl G. Knoob, William J. Lock, Marjorie Mascheroni, John B. Moore, Jr., Arthur Nichols, Ralph D. Ranger, Jr., and Steven Schroeder for their assistance and contributions at various stages of this project.

Photographs are by the author, except as noted.

Sources and References

Robert G. Athearn, *The Denver and Rio Grande Western Railroad* (Lincoln: University of Nebraska Press, 1977).

Gerald M. Best, *Snowplow: Clearing Mountain Rails* (Berkeley: Howell-North Books, 1966).

Thomas M. Lell, "Plowing Through History," *Locomotive & Railway Preservation*, July–August 1992.

Doris B. Osterwald, *Ticket to Toltec* (Lakewood, CO: Western Guideways, Ltd., 1992).

Robert W. Richardson, *Narrow Gauge News* and *Iron Horse News*, various issues, 1957–1980.

Scenic Railways, Inc., *An Illustrated Review of Winter Operations on the C&TSRR*, 1978.

Mike Del Vecchio, "Steam and Snow on Cumbres," *Railfan & Railroad Magazine*, August 1993.

Since it was formed in 1970, the Cumbres & Toltec Scenic Railroad has on six occasions used rotary snowplow OY to clear its track of accumulated snow over 10,015-foot Cumbres Pass. These rotary operations have been conducted in the springtime, usually to open the railroad for the summer excursion season. Taken on May 4, 1991, this photograph shows OY working up the 4 percent grade on the west side of Cumbres Pass. The dense, wet, springtime snowpack, up to fourteen feet deep in places, will give the rotary and its crew a vigorous workout. At the location shown in this photograph, about a mile and a half below Cumbres, the snow is only about a foot deep; the deep snow and about two hours of difficult plowing are still ahead. Photograph by James P. Bell, copyright 1991.

INTRODUCTION

The purpose of this book is to illustrate the operation of two historic rotary snowplows owned by the Cumbres & Toltec Scenic Railroad. The C&TS's rotary snowplows are steam-powered machines designed to remove snow from railroad track in much the same fashion as a modern snow-blower, although the technology of the rotary plow dates from the 1880s.

Between 1974 and 1994, the C&TS has operated its rotaries on several occasions, either as public demonstrations, for filming television commercials, or to clear the track over Cumbres Pass of accumulated snow. On one occasion, in May 1993, four days were required to clear the C&TS track of snow, in order to open the railroad for the summer passenger season.

The track that today comprises the C&TS was built in 1880 by the Denver & Rio Grande Railway. The D&RG had been organized in 1870 to build a railroad line from Denver, Colorado, to El Paso, Texas. The company's promoters, influenced by economies achieved in the construction of narrow gauge railroads in Great Britain, decided the new railroad would also be narrow gauge. A track gauge of 36 inches was chosen, rather than the standard track gauge of 56½ inches. Construction began at Denver in 1871. Five years later, the railroad had progressed south to the vicinity of Trinidad, Colorado.

By the late 1870s, the booming mining camps in the Rocky Mountains seemed to offer the D&RG more lucrative sources of traffic than did the distant goal of El Paso. Thus, in 1876 twenty-two miles of track were built to La Veta, Colorado, the beginning of an extension into the San Luis Valley and, eventually, to Durango and Silverton, Colorado. Two years later, the company started work on a branch to the rich Leadville, Colorado, mining district.

Events then intervened to end the company's plans of a railroad to El Paso. Raton Pass, over which the D&RG had

D&RG rotary OM pauses while clearing the main track at Cumbres, Colorado, probably in February or March 1909. The plow, facing east in this photograph, apparently has worked up the 4 percent grade on the west side of Cumbres Pass. In the left background, above the last locomotive, can be seen a portion of the snowshed covering the wye at Cumbres. One of the workmen standing on the track in front of the rotary wields a sledgehammer with which he has been breaking compacted snow and ice loose from the rotary's wheel. Photograph by Monte Ballough, collection of Ernest W. Robart.

planned to build its track into New Mexico, was occupied by the Atchison, Topeka & Santa Fe Railroad. The Santa Fe also began a railroad to Leadville. The route to Leadville selected by both companies followed the Arkansas River, passing through the Royal Gorge. But the Royal Gorge was not wide enough to accommodate two railroads, and a complicated struggle ensued that was fought both in the courts and on the ground. Finally, in March 1880, an agreement was reached whereby, for a period of ten years, the Rio Grande agreed to build no farther south than Española, New Mexico, and the Santa Fe agreed to stay out of Denver and Leadville. Although its branch to Española was completed in December 1880, and the Santa Fe broke the agreement by building to Denver in 1887, the D&RG's future lay to the west.

The D&RG's San Juan Extension from Antonito to Silverton, Colorado, was completed in 1882. Between Antonito and Chama, New Mexico, track built in 1880 crossed Cumbres Pass at an elevation of 10,015 feet. Between Salida and Grand Junction, Colorado,

another narrow gauge mainline built in 1881 that headed for Salt Lake City crossed Marshall Pass at an elevation of 10,860 feet. The Rio Grande had become a mountain railroad.

The narrow gauge track proved well-suited to construction in difficult mountainous terrain. Because the small equipment could negotiate sharp curves, grading and construction costs were reduced. In the winter, though, the locomotives then used, weighing about 35 tons, were often no match for the heavy mountain snows. These locomotives, with wedge plows fitted to their pilots, were often inadequate for clearing snow-filled cuts or drifts of ten feet or more. Trains became stranded in the snow. Snowsheds to protect the track from the snow were constructed at many points, but these were often drifted in as well. In the summer,

snowsheds were vulnerable to fires started by sparks from the locomotives.

By the late 1880s, a remedy to the snow blockades was available — the rotary snowplow, which employed a wheel arrangement to cut into the snow and then throw it away from the track. The rotary snowplow had been developed by Orange Jull of Ontario, Canada, in the mid 1880s. John and Edward Leslie, also of Ontario, acquired Jull's rights, made certain improvements, and organized the Leslie Brothers Manufacturing Co. to market the machine.

Despite the name of their company, the Leslies did not build rotary snowplows; instead, they contracted with locomotive builders, usually the Cooke Locomotive & Machine Works, of Paterson, New Jersey, to construct the machines. The Leslies also located their office in Paterson, where Cooke and several other locomotive manufacturers, potential builders of rotary snowplows, had their factories. In 1901, the American Locomotive Co. was organized to consolidate Cooke with a number of other builders. John Leslie, the surviving brother, transferred the right to build rotary snowplows to the new company. Consequently, after 1903, rotary snowplows were built by the American Locomotive Company or its licensees. Most of the American Locomotive Company's rotaries were produced at the Cooke Works, until the plant was closed in 1926.

Rotary snowplow at work on the east side of Cumbres Pass, February 1909. The machine pictured here is rotary snowplow no. 2 of the Rio Grande Southern Railroad. The RGS, also a three-foot gauge railroad, was completed in 1891 between Durango and Ridgway, Colorado, both points being junctions with the D&RG's narrow gauge lines. Rotary no. 2 was built the following year, one of two such machines owned by the RGS. It was badly damaged by a boiler explosion in 1949 and subsequently scrapped. In this view, the rotary is plowing west near milepost 330, approaching the east switch at Cumbres. Its presence on the D&RG shows that, on occasion, the Rio Grande's rotaries needed assistance fighting the winter snow blockades. Photograph by Monte Ballough, collection of Ernest W. Robart.

Cumbres & Toltec rotary snowplow OM, the older of two such machines owned by the railroad, works its way through a snowdrift near the west end of Cresco siding, about eight miles north of Chama, New Mexico, in March 1975. OM was used by the C&TS on four occasions from 1974 to 1976. Photograph by Clif Palmer.

CUMBRES & TOLTEC ROTARY SNOWPLOWS

The Rio Grande owned four narrow gauge rotary plows, designated OM, ON, OO, and OY. Rotary OM, delivered as no. 1 but later renumbered, was completed by the Cooke Locomotive & Machine Works in February 1889. This rotary survives today on the Cumbres & Toltec Scenic Railroad. Rotary ON, delivered as no. 2, was completed by the Cooke Works in March 1889. It was sold to the War Department during World War II and was shipped to Alaska for use on the White Pass & Yukon Railroad. This machine was used as rip rap alongside the Skagway River in 1968. Rotary OO, built by Cooke for the Colorado Fuel & Iron Company in 1900, was acquired by the Rio Grande in 1920. Assigned to Gunnison, Colorado, for use over Marshall Pass, OO was scrapped after 1955, following abandonment of the Marshall Pass line. In November 1923, the D&RG acquired its fourth and last narrow gauge rotary, OY, which today is also preserved on the Cumbres & Toltec. Rotary OY was built at the American Locomotive Company's Cooke Works.

In later years, both OM and OY were assigned to the Alamosa–Chama line. As the more modern and slightly larger of the two rotaries, OY was preferred. Operationally, it was easier to plow west from Alamosa to Cumbres against a ruling grade of 1.42 percent than up the 4 percent grade from Chama to Cumbres. Thus, OY was stored in the roundhouse at Alamosa, while OM was kept in Chama.

In the late 1920s, the Denver & Rio Grande Western Railroad (successor in a 1921 reorganization to the Denver & Rio Grande Railway) acquired its class K-36 and K-37 locomotives (numbered 480–489 and 490–499, respectively). These locomotives weighed about 90 tons. When equipped with pilot plows, they were much more effective at snow removal than the earlier, smaller motive power. Snow up to about six feet deep could be handled without firing up one of the rotaries. Daily train service also helped keep the tracks clear of snow, although severe storms would occasionally leave enough snow that the rotaries would be

needed to open the railroad.

The Rio Grande last used rotary OM in late January 1957, when two locomotives equipped with pilot plows were dispatched from Chama during a heavy storm to plow the track to Cumbres. After one of the locomotives derailed at Cumbres, another train was sent to bring the crew of the first train back to Chama. This second train became stuck in the snow a short distance west of the pass. To rescue the train, OM, pushed by three locomotives, was sent up the pass from Chama. The second train, stalled below Windy Point, was extricated.

Further progress toward Cumbres by the rotary train was blocked by a snow slide. While the rotary worked to clear this slide, snow drifted in behind the train, stranding the plow and the three locomotives. Consequently, OY was dispatched west from Alamosa. Progress

Cumbres & Toltec Scenic Railroad locomotive 487, with a snowplow mounted on its pilot (487 has been equipped with a pilot plow since the 1960s). When equipped with such plows, the Denver & Rio Grande Western's 2-8-2 locomotives could clear fresh snow drifts up to five or six feet deep from the track.

was slow. The OY reached Cumbres on February 2, seven days after the storm began. Workers stranded at Cumbres had been rescued the day before by helicopter and by Army snow vehicles.

Rotary OY was last used by the Rio Grande five years later. On March 28, 1962, OY arrived in Chama after plowing west from Antonito. In subsequent years, snow conditions did not require further use of either OM or OY. Drifts too deep for the locomotives to clear could be opened with bulldozers, carried on flatcars as part of a plow train. Also, after the mid 1960s, declining traffic reduced the need to keep the line open over Cumbres Pass. Traffic could be diverted to the highway when snow conditions made train operation hazardous.

The last winter operation over Cumbres occurred on January, 26, 1966, when locomotives 493 and 483, with Jordan spreader OU (also now on the C&TS), ran from Chama to Alamosa. The next train over Cumbres was not until May 1966.

Finally, on July 25, 1969, the Interstate Commerce Commission approved the Rio Grande's request to abandon the narrow gauge line over Cumbres Pass. That year and the next, a small group of dedicated volunteers began working to save part of the narrow gauge. Their efforts resulted in the states of Colorado and New Mexico purchasing that portion of the railroad between Antonito and Chama. Included in the purchase were nine locomotives and thirty pieces of nonrevenue equipment. Among the latter were rotary snowplows OM and OY (both had been maintained in a serviceable condition by the Rio Grande). The track and equipment constitute what is today operated as the Cumbres & Toltec Scenic Railroad.

Cumbres & Toltec Scenic Railroad rotary OY, formerly Denver & Rio Grande Western OY, at Cumbres, Colorado, April 22, 1978. OY has been repainted by the C&TS to the boxcar-red color applied to Rio Grande work equipment before World War II. OY weighs 148,000 pounds; its wheel is nine feet, eight and one-half inches in diameter. Photograph by Tom Klinger.

Denver & Rio Grande Western rotary OM at Chama, New Mexico, June 1967. The plow is painted gray with black lettering, the color scheme applied in later years by the railroad to its nonrevenue equipment. OM, minus its tender, weighs 132,480 pounds in working order. The diameter of the wheel is nine feet, two inches. OM is now owned by the C&TS.

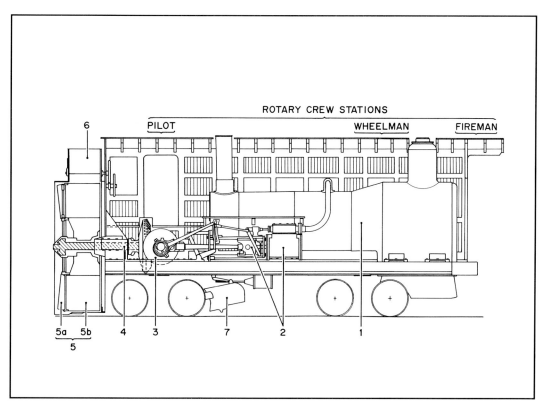

ROTARY CREW STATIONS

The carbody of a rotary snowplow encloses a boiler (1); steam from the boiler is fed to a reciprocating steam engine (2), which drives a pair of gears (3). These gears, one on each side of the mechanism, drive a third gear, which is attached to a longitudinal shaft (4). Connected to this shaft is the rotary wheel (5), which comprises two blades: a snow cutting blade (5a), which slices into the snow as the rotary advances, and a fan blade (5b). The fan blade, a series of hollow rectangular or, as in later rotaries such as OY, conical shapes, receives snow from the cutting blade and discharges it through a chute (6) at the top of the wheel's hood. The chute can be tilted to discharge the snow to either the right or left of the plow. Behind the front truck, a flanger blade (7) may be lowered to clear the remaining few inches of snow from between the rails. A rotary snowplow is not self-propelled; the boiler generates steam solely to operate the rotary wheel. The rotary is pushed through the snow by one or more locomotives.

The interior of C&TS rotary snowplow OM. This photograph, which looks forward from the wheelman's position, shows the close working area inside the rotary. The vertical lever at the lower center foreground of the photograph is the throttle, which controls the amount of steam admitted to the rotary's cylinders; projecting down at an angle from the left foreground is the reverse lever, used to control the direction in which the wheel rotates. When the plow is operating, the crew members must coordinate their actions in the environment of noise, heat, and vibration generated by the rotary's reciprocating steam machinery. Photograph by Ernest W. Robart, January 11, 1974.

Rotary Snowplow Operation
Earl G. Knoob
Safety & Compliance Officer/Superintendent of Operations, Cumbres & Toltec Scenic Railroad

Operating a rotary snowplow is very much a team effort. In addition to the operation of the rotary plow itself, the efforts of the locomotives pushing the plow have to be coordinated for the best results. If one locomotive tries to push harder than the others, the result is usually lots of drive-wheel slips and, perhaps, even running out of water and coal at a very inopportune moment.

The rotary plow itself carries a crew of four or five: pilot, wheelman (or rotary engineer), two firemen, and sometimes the roadmaster or track foreman rides in the pilothouse. The pilot rides up in the front of the plow — the pilothouse is right behind the rotary wheel. Because the pilot, in theory, has the best view, he is in charge of coordinating the entire operation. He communicates with the locomotive engineers by whistle signals: one blast on the whistle means "Stop," two mean "Ahead," three mean "Back Up," if stopped, or "Slow Down," if moving. The pilot also decides to which side of the track the snow is to be thrown, and he controls the hood that directs the snow to one side of the track or the other. The pilot also controls the air brakes on the train.

The rotary wheel clears snow to about four inches from the top of the rail. To remove the remaining snow and ice from above the rail, and to clear the flangeways inside of

and below the tops of the rails, a small flanger blade is attached to the rotary's front truck. This blade is raised or lowered by an air-operated cylinder; it is lowered to remove snow or raised so that switches, road crossings, and cattle guards aren't damaged. The flanger blade is usually operated by the roadmaster or track foreman.

The wheelman runs the plow's wheel. He is stationed alongside the boiler, about two-thirds of the way back. In that position, with very little visibility, he relies on the pilot for instructions. The pilot communicates to the wheelman using a signal bell. One ding means "Stop," two dings mean "Go," and three

dings mean "Slow Down." Many times the pilot and wheelman rely on hand signals because the noise in the rotary can drown out all other sounds — other than screaming into the other guy's ear!

The wheelman's controls are similar to those of a steam locomotive. There are a throttle and reverse levers for speed and direction control — although on a rotary the reverse lever is used to throw the snow either to the left or right of the track. The wheelman also has a steam gauge and, behind him, a gauge glass so that he can see how much water is in the boiler.

The duties of the two firemen are the same as those on board a locomotive — to maintain the steam pressure and the water level in the boiler. Because the rotary is run so hard when clearing snow, vast amounts of coal and water are consumed. To plow the track from Chama to Cumbres, OY will use about 10,000 gallons of water and six to eight tons of coal. This incredible appetite for coal and water makes it almost impossible for one man to fire the rotary all day long. So, to keep from killing the fireman,

The rotary train as seen by the pilot. This view was taken while OY was engaged in clearing a deep drift near milepost 336, just below Cresco, Colorado, on May 3, 1993. Photograph by Earl G. Knoob.

two firemen are used.

The firemen are usually seen in the gangway between the rotary's tender and the boiler backhead, where the firebox door is located. Also on the backhead is a water glass and a steam gauge so that the firemen can monitor the boiler. Injectors that supply water to the boiler are located on each side of the boiler, just inside the carbody, ahead of the gangway. The left injector draws its water from the tender, and the right injector draws its water from the auxiliary water tank behind the tender.

When approaching a snowdrift, the pilot signals the locomotives to slow down to a walk (three toots on the whistle). About ten feet from the snow, he signals the wheelman to start the blade (two dings on the communication bell). The wheelman cracks the throttle open and moves the reverse lever up to about one-third of the way from the center notch on the quadrant. As the plow bites into the snow, the pilot again signals the wheelman "Go," for more power to the wheel.

Usually, as the rotary begins clearing snow, the plow train's forward progress is halted. Then, the locomotive engineers open their throt-

tles to keep moving ahead. If too much throttle is used, the wheel will stall; if not enough throttle is used, the rotary wheel will not bite into the snow — it will polish a nice face into the snow that the wheel can't bite into effectively.

Once into the snow, the speed at which the plow blade rotates is controlled by either the throttle or the reverse lever. Usually, if the snow depth is more than four feet, the throttle is opened wide and the speed is controlled by the reverse lever. As plowing proceeds, the locomotive engineers maintain a steady walking pace. If the rotary is pushed into a drift faster than it can chew up the snow and discharge it to the side, the wheel will begin to bog down. Sometimes, when this happens, the increased drag of snow not being discharged will slow the train. When the excess snow is chewed up and thrown off to the side, train speed will pick up again.

The locomotive engineers must be alert to the speed variations. When the train speed begins to drop, they must not open their throttles until forward motion stops — as soon as the rotary wheel clears out the extra snow, train speed will pick up. Opening the locomotive throttles as the train speed drops would simply push the plow harder into the snow, probably stalling the wheel. If it stalls, the rotary must be backed out of the snow and the wheel cleared by opening the rotary throttle and spinning the wheel to clear the packed snow. Sometimes the wheel is packed so solidly that it must be spun in reverse to break the snow loose. Once the wheel is clear, plowing may be resumed.

Riding on the rotary is a truly unique experience, and not one for the faint at heart. The whole rotary train takes on an odd forward-and-back motion while plowing. In addition, the plow itself bucks up and down three to six inches while plowing — and the cylinders and rods on the rotary are right under the pilot's feet. When the rotary is working hard, every stroke of the pistons can be felt through the floor of the pilothouse. Hanging on for dear life to whatever is bolted down is a must. The notion that the rotary was on the verge of coming apart at the seams has crossed my mind more than a few times. The smokestack on the rotary is located about five feet behind the pilothouse, making the exhaust deafening. Also, the rapid exhaust of the rotary takes on a very irritating whistling sound when working wide open in deep, hard snow. Even with ear plugs, one's ears can be ringing by the end of the day — let alone after four days! Adding all this together makes working on the rotary an exciting proposition.

The view from rotary OY's pilot house, taken near milepost 336 on May 3, 1993. While clearing this drift, the snow stalled the rotary wheel; the plow has been pulled back from the drift so that packed snow can be cleared from the wheel. The face of the snowdrift, which has been polished by the rotary's snow-cutting blade, will be more difficult for the blade to cut into when plowing resumes. The crest of the drift is being shoveled off to alleviate resistance to the snow-cutting blade when plowing resumes. Photograph by Earl G. Knoob.

Rotary snowplow OM in the yard at Chama, New Mexico, on the evening of February 14, 1976. The next day, OM, pushed by locomotives 487 and 483, plowed north from Chama for about four miles—the third of four Winter Specials operated by the C&TS in the 1970s. Photograph by George Lawrence, lighting by Mallory Hope Ferrell.

ROTARY OPERATIONS
1974–1980

In 1971, the Cumbres & Toltec was leased to Scenic Railways, Inc., for excursion operation. These excursions were limited to the summer tourist season, and no attempt was made to operate trains during the winter. Encouraging growth in ridership was experienced during the first two years of operation. This progress was interrupted in 1973 when reports of fuel shortages caused many vacationers to forego travel in the Rocky Mountain West. The imposition of the Arab oil embargo in September 1973 suggested, correctly, that the 1974 season would be no improvement. The number of passengers riding the C&TS in 1973 fell so low that operation of the railroad in 1974 was placed in doubt.

Against this background, sentiment grew among the employees of Scenic Railways to operate a rotary snowplow during the 1973–1974 winter. If excursion operations could not be resumed in 1974, a rotary train would at least provide a spectacular finale to Scenic Railway's efforts. It might be the last opportunity for one of the historic snowplows to operate.

Rotary OM was in Chama — where it had been stationed since the 1920s — so that machine was chosen for the operation. The OY, though newer, was at the time stored in Antonito; the railroad's serviceable locomotives were kept in Chama during the winter. Separated by Cumbres Pass and the winter snowpack from the locomotives, OY was not available for use.

Scenic's employees examined OM and found that it could be returned to operation with only minor repairs. Based on OM's good condition, a test run of the plow was scheduled for January 12, 1974.

Repairs were made, and OM was successfully fired up on January 10, 1974. Two days later, as scheduled, OM and locomotive 487 cleared the track of about three feet of snow for a distance of about two miles north from Chama. Though the event was not advertised, news of the planned operation spread. Many people traveled to Chama to witness the event; about forty were able to ride in an open gondola behind 487. Thus, the 1974 operation became the first of four Winter Specials operated by Scenic Railways.

Subsequent Winter Specials in 1975 and 1976 also featured OM. No operation occurred in 1977. The time and labor needed to prepare for and operate the Specials was largely contributed by Scenic's employees on a volunteer basis. After three consecutive winters of rotary snowplow operations, the employees decided a respite was in order for the winter of 1977–1978.

What showed signs of becoming an annual event was resumed in 1978. This time rotary OY was used. The plow had been moved to Chama from Antonito in October 1977, and necessary repairs were made. The advancing age of OM, nearly ninety years old in 1978, made the use of OY desirable. On February 4, OY and locomotive 487 plowed tracks in the Chama yard. The following day, 487 pushed the rotary north out of Chama, clearing the track for about three miles. This was OY's first operation since 1962.

Later, in April 1978, OY was used to clear snow from the track over Cumbres Pass. Previously, none of the C&TS rotary trains had proceeded beyond Cresco, Colorado, about nine miles above Chama. The April 1978 train was the first operation of a rotary over the pass since 1962. A motion picture was to be filmed on the C&TS in the vicinity of Antonito; the rotary snowplow was used to open the railroad so that equipment to be used in the filming could be moved to Antonito from Chama. The plow train worked east to the Rock Tunnel at mile 315.2, then returned to Chama. The plowing required three days. A similar operation took place in 1980, but the event was not documented photographically.

Kyle Railways succeeded Scenic Railways as operator of the C&TS in 1982. By then, the scale of summer excursion traffic was beginning to stretch the limits of available equipment. During the winter, the railroad's labor, funds, and shop space were needed to prepare locomotives and passenger cars for the forthcoming season. Both OM and OY were operable, but there were no plans to repeat any of the Winter Specials. As events developed, however, Kyle Railways has had to operate OY as far east as Osier, Colorado, on several occasions.

1974 Winter Special

The yard at Chama, New Mexico, on the morning of January 11, 1974. The yard tracks, covered by about three feet of snow, were plowed out by locomotive 487 equipped with a pilot plow; rotary OM is under steam, ready for use the following day. Photograph by Ernest W. Robart.

On the morning of January 12, 1974, 487 eases rotary OM past the Chama water tank. After 487 takes on water, the plow train will proceed north from Chama. Photograph by Tom Klinger.

Rotary OM working out of the north end of the Chama yard, January 12, 1974. Photograph by William Moyers, Jr.

Plowing about eighteen inches of powdery, mid-winter snow near mile 342.5, January 12, 1974. Photograph by William Moyers, Jr.

In The Narrows, the track closely parallels Highway 17, from which this view of the rotary was taken. Photograph by Ernest W. Robart.

Near mile 341.5, plowing was suspended. After this photograph was taken, the train backed into Chama, completing the first of four Winter Specials. Photograph by Ernest W. Robart.

1975 Winter Special

The success of the 1974 rotary operation prompted the C&TS to repeat the event in 1975, 1976, and 1978. Each operation was conducted as a public event—not as an operational necessity to open the railroad for traffic. Thus, on none of these occasions did the plow trains operate more than a few miles north of Chama.

The 1975 Winter Special was initially scheduled for January 11 and 12. Because a dry winter left insufficient snow, the event was rescheduled for the first and second of February. Even then, there was barely enough snow to operate the rotary. To reach snow of some depth and provide the rotary an opportunity to do some plowing, the plow train ran north of Lobato Trestle—a little over four miles above Chama and the farthest point reached by any of the Winter Specials.

The equipment used by the 1975 plow train was selected to represent a rotary train such as the Rio Grande might have operated. Trailing 487 was car 053, a former Railway Post Office car converted by the D&RGW for use by the rotary crew. Next came an outfit car, such as might have been used by workmen accompanying the train or by other crew members. Caboose 0503 was the last car.

The 1975 Winter Special on the flats north of Chama, February 1, 1975. Photographs by Darrell T. Arndt.

16

Entering The Narrows, about two miles north of Chama, the train encountered the start of the 4 percent grade to Cumbres. About half a mile beyond the point shown in this view, 487 stalled on icy rails. As it was by then late in the afternoon, plowing was suspended. The equipment returned to Chama for the night. Photograph by Darrell T. Arndt.

A second attempt to run OM at least as far as Lobato was made on February 2, 1975. In this view, OM, pushed by locomotive 487, eases past the Chama coaling tower on its way out of the yard. This was the second day of the 1975 Winter Special. Only a few inches of snow covered the ground in Chama, in contrast to about three feet of snow the previous year, as shown in the photographs on page 14. Photograph by Darrell T. Arndt.

LEFT and ABOVE: The rails were still icy on the 2nd, preventing the single locomotive from moving the plow train up the 4 percent grade. To lighten the train, the cars behind the locomotive were uncoupled; 487 was then able to push OM and water car 0471 over the snow-covered track. In these views, OM and 487 exit The Narrows, about one-half mile below Lobato, February 2, 1975. Photographs by Darrell T. Arndt.

17

ABOVE and LEFT: After crossing Lobato Trestle, the plow train proceeded through fresh, powdery snow for a further half mile before returning to Chama. Photographs by Clif Palmer.

To reach locations with more snow to plow, the rotary train ventured another two and one-half miles beyond The Narrows, reaching some drifts above Lobato Trestle. Here, OM and 487 are approaching Lobato Trestle, February 2, 1975. Photograph by Clif Palmer.

Opening the Railroad Chama to Cresco February 1975

Two weeks after 1975's Winter Special, the C&TS ran OM to clear the track as far as Cresco, Colorado, nine miles from Chama. The railroad had contracted to operate a train for the filming of a television commercial. The rotary did not appear in the commercial, but its use was necessary to plow drifts that covered the track to depths of up to six feet. The effort consumed two days.

RIGHT: Locomotive 487 pushes rotary OM out of The Narrows. This part of the railroad had been plowed during the Winter Special, but later storms had deposited fresh snow on the track. Photograph by Clif Palmer.

BELOW: Working through about a foot of snow near Dalton, five miles above Chama. Photograph by Clif Palmer.

The photographs above and to the lower left illustrate the ability of the rotary pilot to direct the snow to either side of the track. Generally, the snow is directed to the downhill side. In the upper view, exiting The Narrows, the downhill side is to the left side of the rotary. Above Lobato, as in the lower view, the downhill side is to the right, or engineer's, side of the plow.

At Dalton, the railroad crosses Forest Road 121; this crossing was shoveled out by the track crew to remove any ice that might have accumulated in the flangeways. Photograph by Clif Palmer.

On the second day, 487 and OM are shown near milepost 338, above Dalton. Deeper drifts were encountered further up the track as the plow neared Cresco. Photograph by Clif Palmer.

ABOVE and LEFT: OM works through a six-foot drift near milepost 336, about half a mile below the east end of Cresco siding. Photographs by Clif Palmer.

Accompanied by a solitary cross-country skier, OM approaches its goal, the water tank at Cresco, Colorado. It was not necessary to plow farther, so after reaching the tank, 487 and OM returned to Chama. Photograph by Clif Palmer.

1976 Winter Special

BELOW LEFT: Rotary OM's last operation occurred during the Winter Special of February 1976. After the experience of the previous year, when a single locomotive had been found inadequate to power the train, it was decided that two engines would be employed. This view shows the plow, with locomotives 487 and 483, in the Chama yard on the morning of February 15, 1976. A light snow is falling. Photograph by Tom Klinger.

OPPOSITE and BELOW RIGHT: Rotary OM plows past the Chama water tank and through the switch at the north end of the yard — for the benefit of the many onlookers. Photographs by Ernest W. Robart.

ABOVE and BELOW: The plow train exits The Narrows, just above milepost 341, February 15, 1976. One hundred and eighteen passengers rode in the cars behind locomotive 483. Photographs by Ernest W. Robart.

ABOVE: The 1976 Winter Special operated as far as the Lobato siding, about four miles above Chama. In this view, at Lobato, the train has stopped; the locomotives will be uncoupled and the equipment backed into Chama. Photograph by Ernest W. Robart.

BELOW: Locomotive 483 has uncoupled and, with the outfit cars and caboose, has backed into Chama. In this view, 487 is easing rotary OM back to the yard as well. For safety such reverse moves involving more than one locomotive are made with each locomotive operating independently. Photograph by Tom Klinger.

1978 Winter Special

After a year's rest from winter operations, the C&TS operated a last Winter Special in February 1978. It featured rotary OY, steamed up for its first operation since 1962. The event occupied two days, February 4 and 5. On the 4th, OY was used to plow out some of the Chama yard tracks. Then, the railroad's Jordan spreader OU was used over the track between the north end of the yard and the Highway 17 road crossing north of town. The Rio Grande had often used the spreader, coupled behind a locomotive, to keep the line over Cumbres Pass open during the winter. The following day, OY plowed to a point about three miles north of Chama.

Rotary OY plows a few inches of snow from the main track at the north end of the yard in Chama, on February 4, 1978. Photograph by Ernest W. Robart.

ABOVE: On the afternoon of February 4, the use of a spreader to clear snow from the track was demonstrated. In snow removal work when a rotary was not required, the D&RGW often used spreader OU behind a locomotive equipped with a pilot plow. The locomotive would break through the drifts, and the spreader, with its wings extended, would push the snow away from the track. By thus widening the snow cut, the spreader would make it easier to plow drifts left by subsequent storms. In this view, 487 and OU are shown just north of the Highway 17 crossing, near mile 343.5. Photograph by Ernest W. Robart.

RIGHT: Rotary OY and the plow train at Chama on the morning of February 5, 1978. Besides the rotary and locomotive 487, the train included a gondola, an excursion car, and caboose 05635. Photograph by Ernest W. Robart.

24

Plowing across the flats about a mile north of Chama, February 5, 1978. Photograph by Ernest W. Robart.

BELOW LEFT and RIGHT: Rotary OY at work in The Narrows, about two and one-half miles north of Chama. The train operated about another half mile before returning to the yard. Photographs by Ernest W. Robart.

Opening the Railroad April 1978

The first operation of a rotary plow over Cumbres Pass by the C&TS took place in April 1978. Motion picture footage, including train operations, was to be filmed on the railroad west of Antonito, Colorado. Because the filming was to be accomplished before the opening of the excursion season, the necessary equipment, stored in Chama over the winter, had to be moved to Antonito. To open the railroad for that purpose, rotary OY was employed. Locomotives 487 and 484 powered the train.

The first plowing occurred near milepost 336, just below the siding at Cresco, Colorado, where the track crosses the Colorado-New Mexico state line. The OY, 487, and 484 are shown here working through about a foot of snow, April 21, 1978. Photograph by George Lawrence.

On April 21, OY ran from Chama to Cumbres. Between The Narrows and Lobato, track over which the Winter Special had operated two months earlier, only a few patches of snow remained on the ground. Photograph by George Lawrence.

Above Cresco tank, occasional drifts of three to four feet covered the track. In this view, the train has backed away from one of the drifts so that OY's wheel could be cleared of the dense, wet, springtime snow. Photograph by George Lawrence.

In an attempt to keep the track clear of drifted snow, the D&RG constructed snowsheds at numerous locations between Cresco and Osier. The last of these snowsheds covered the wye at Cumbres Pass. Until the winter of 1978–1979, the snowshed at Cumbres was largely intact, though decrepit. That winter, after decades without maintenance, most of the shed collapsed under the weight of accumulated snow. As a safety measure, the remainder of the snowshed, except for a short portion over the tail of the wye, was torn down during the summer of 1979. Recently, the Friends of the C&TS has begun a long-term project to rebuild the Cumbres snowshed.

On the morning of April 22, 1978, OY and the plow train sit on the siding at Cumbres; a portion of the snowshed appears behind the rotary. Photograph by Tom Klinger.

Upon reaching Cumbres, Colorado, on the afternoon of April 21, 1978, OY proceeded to clear out the side tracks at that point. This photograph shows the plow working up to the snowshed which, at that time, covered most of the west leg of the wye. Photograph by George Lawrence.

TOP and BOTTOM LEFT. On the morning of April 22, plowing began to open the track east of Cumbres. These views show rotary OY plowing across the fill over Cumbres Creek, about a mile and a half east of the summit, April 22, 1978. Photographs by George Lawrence.

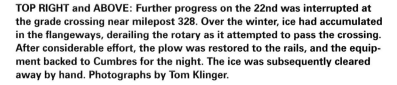

TOP RIGHT and ABOVE: Further progress on the 22nd was interrupted at the grade crossing near milepost 328. Over the winter, ice had accumulated in the flangeways, derailing the rotary as it attempted to pass the crossing. After considerable effort, the plow was restored to the rails, and the equipment backed to Cumbres for the night. The ice was subsequently cleared away by hand. Photographs by Tom Klinger.

Work resumed on April 23 to clear the track east of milepost 328. These three views show OY and the two locomotives plowing through a light covering of snow near milepost 327. Photographs by Tom Klinger.

Approaching Los Pinos tank
on the afternoon of April 23,
1978. Photograph by
Tom Klinger.

Rotary snowplow OY and
locomotives 487 and 484
stopped for water at Los
Pinos tank, April 23, 1978.
Photograph by Tom Klinger.

Beyond Los Pinos, plowing
continued as far as Rock
Tunnel, mile 315.2. From the
tunnel, the rotary train continued east to Antonito,
where it remained over-
night. The equipment re-
turned to Chama on April
24, completing the C&TS's
first rotary operation over
Cumbres Pass.

1979 Television Commercial

After opening the track over Cumbres Pass in April 1978, OY's next use was in March 1979. The rotary was employed in filming a television commercial for a brewing company.

The scene in the yard at Chama on March 15, 1979, as the equipment is readied for filming. Photograph by James P. Bell, copyright 1979.

Rotary OY plowing east from Cumbres, Colorado, at milepost 329, on May 25, 1983.

OPENING THE RAILROAD
1983

On May 25 and 26, 1983, the Cumbres & Toltec operated rotary snowplow OY to clear the railroad for opening on June 4. Exceptionally frequent and late spring snow storms left deep drifts on the line between Coxo and Windy Point, waist-deep snow at Cumbres, and frequent drifts between Cumbres and Osier.

The rotary operation was undertaken only when it became clear that the cool spring weather would keep snow on the track past the opening date. With two engine crews, a rotary crew, a crew to dig out switches, and other necessary support, it was an expensive operation. The cost was partially offset by extensive media attention, including nationally broadcast television coverage.

The rotary train consisted of rotary OY, auxiliary water car 0471, locomotives 487 and 488, an outfit car, and caboose 0503. The train departed for Cumbres about 10:30 a.m. on the 25th. The first snow was encountered above Cresco, and at the grade crossing below Coxo the snow was two to three feet deep. That crossing was reached about noon, where a stop of an hour or so was made for lunch.

When plowing resumed, the snow presented no particular difficulty until within about half a mile of Windy Point. There, two long, deep drifts, reaching to the top of the rotary hood and composed of heavy, wet snow, greatly restricted plowing. Through the deepest portions of these drifts, progress of a foot or so would be made before the train would back up, clear the rotary blade of compacted snow, and then advance once more.

Windy Point itself was mostly clear of snow. At Cumbres the depth was two to four feet. Most of the afternoon was consumed in watering the locomotives and rotary, then clearing the siding and one leg of the wye. To plow these other tracks, it was first necessary to shovel out the switches by hand.

After the tracks at Cumbres were opened, work resumed on clearing the track to the east of the pass; much of the track as far east as milepost 329 was covered by drifted snow. One or two more drifts, about three miles east of Cumbres, also were plowed that afternoon. The train then backed to Cumbres, tying up for the night at about 5:30 p.m.

An early start was contemplated for the next morning. Servicing of the equipment started about 7:30 a.m. A supply of coal had earlier been positioned along the highway at Cumbres, and a front-end loader was employed to load this coal into the tenders. The only place free of snow for the loader to operate was the highway crossing. Although highway traffic was not heavy, the train had to back free of the crossing so that occasional vehicles could pass. About 9:30 a.m., servicing was completed and plowing resumed. Drifts of two to three feet were encountered between milepost 328 and Los Pinos tank. Los Pinos loop was free of snow, but across the valley snow still covered portions of the track. The plow train worked as far east as Osier, clearing a big drift at that point.

Taking water at Chama, New Mexico, just before leaving for Cumbres, May 25, 1983. The OY's tender holds 5,000 gallons of water; the auxiliary water car behind the tender holds another 6,000 gallons. Between Chama and Cumbres, OY will consume about 10,000 gallons of water.

The 1983 rotary train was composed of OY, auxiliary water car 0471, locomotives 487 and 488, outfit car 04982, and caboose 0503. The location is in The Narrows — where much of the plowing was accomplished during the Winter Specials of the 1970s. This photograph may be compared with one on page 25 taken at the same location in 1978.

The rotary above milepost 333, approaching the Highway 17 grade crossing, May 15, 1983. The snow was about a foot deep at this point. Photograph by John Chenowith.

The 1983 trip received much more advance notice than any of the trips since the Winter Specials; accordingly, the event was witnessed by about two hundred people. The press was also on hand for the event — in this view, as OY works across the Highway 17 grade crossing below Coxo, Colorado, a helicopter used by a television news crew waits to the left of the track.

RIGHT and BELOW: Clearing about two feet of snow between Highway 17 and Coxo, May 25, 1983. Photograph below by John Chenowith.

LEFT and BELOW: Above Coxo, working toward Windy Point. Photograph below by John Chenowith.

Cumbres, Colorado, on the afternoon of May 25, 1983. After passing the section house and standpipe at Cumbres, OY plowed the main track as far as the highway crossing before taking water. Photograph by John Chenowith.

The rotary train just below Windy Point, plowing through a drift twelve to fourteen feet deep on May 25, 1983. This drift presented the most difficult obstacle to the rotary's progress toward Cumbres.

RIGHT: In this view, OY emits a smoke ring after stalling in the dense snow covering the track at Cumbres.

LEFT: Rotary OY at the Cumbres section house, May 25, 1983.

After taking water, the plow resumed work to clear the track east of Cumbres. By the end of the day, the track as far east as milepost 328 had been opened. In this view, OY is working down the east side of Cumbres Pass between Tanglefoot Curve and milepost 329.

Plowing east across the fill over Cumbres Creek, approaching milepost 329 on the afternoon of May 25, 1983.

Plowing on May 25 progressed east as far as the Forest Service access road crossing at milepost 328. After clearing this drift, the train returned to Cumbres for the night.

Locomotive 488 taking water at Cumbres on the morning of May 26, 1983.

Heading east across the fill over Cumbres Creek — this track had been cleared on the previous afternoon. Plowing was resumed east of milepost 328.

The equipment at the Highway 17 grade crossing at Cumbres, May 26, 1983. The only clear space available at which coal could be added to the tenders was this road crossing. After the equipment was serviced, the train was reassembled and departed Cumbres to resume plowing.

Drifts between milepost 329 and Los Pinos tank were two to three feet deep. In this view, OY clears about a foot of snow from the track approaching milepost 326.

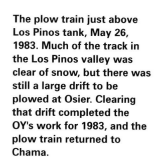

The plow train just above Los Pinos tank, May 26, 1983. Much of the track in the Los Pinos valley was clear of snow, but there was still a large drift to be plowed at Osier. Clearing that drift completed the OY's work for 1983, and the plow train returned to Chama.

Cumbres & Toltec Scenic Railroad rotary OY, pushed by locomotives 487 and 488, approaches the summit of Cumbres Pass during a vigorous snow squall, May 4, 1991. Photograph by Ernest W. Robart.

OPENING THE RAILROAD
1991

The 1983 operation of OY had been undertaken to clear the C&TS track so that excursion operations could begin, as scheduled, in early June that year. By 1991, increased patronage convinced Kyle Railways that excursion trains should begin running on Memorial Day weekend. The expanded season added about ten days to the operating period, but it also increased the chances that a late spring thaw would interfere with the start of scheduled trains.

Such a circumstance in fact occurred the first year of the extended season. By mid-April, deep snow on Cumbres Pass showed no sign of melting away before the scheduled season opening. Accordingly, a decision was reached to once again use OY to clear the track. The plow train was scheduled to operate on May 4 and 5, 1991. As in 1983, the track would be cleared to Cumbres on the first day. On the second day, OY would operate as far east as Osier to finish opening the railroad. Though the rotary operation was expensive, the alternative was to take a chance on delaying the season opening for an unknown number of days.

Based on its 1983 experience, Kyle Railways was again able to take advantage of the free publicity generated by operating a rotary plow. Assisting in this effort was the Friends of the Cumbres & Toltec Scenic Railroad, Inc., an organization of volunteers dedicated to restoring and maintaining the C&TS's historic equipment and structures. The Friends organized a special

passenger excursion to operate in conjunction with the rotary train and prepared press releases to publicize the event. As a result, OY's trip to Cumbres — and the C&TS — again received national attention.

Operationally, the 1991 event was much the same as 1983's. After diligent efforts, taking about a month, C&TS employees readied OY and locomotives 487 and 488 (the same locomotives used in 1983) for the trip. The train departed Chama about 10:00 a.m. on May 4, clearing the track to Cumbres that day.

Snow conditions in 1991 differed from those of 1983. Heavy and wet, as eight years earlier, the 1991 snowpack was topped by an icy crust. This crust seemed more apt to clog the rotary wheel, occasionally stalling OY in drifts not much over three feet deep. The drifts between Coxo and Windy Point, which were deeper and longer than in 1983, greatly slowed the plow train — progress through the deepest drift, roughly at mile 331.25, was often measured in inches. Over an hour's time was required to clear this drift, the top of which on the uphill side was higher than the rotary's roof. In all, about three hours were needed to plow the track from the Highway 17 crossing below Coxo to the section house at Cumbres.

Weather on the morning of May 4 consisted of broken clouds. These developed into vigorous snow squalls as the day progressed. This wintry weather added considerably to the spectacle as OY chewed its

way toward the summit.

After reaching Cumbres Pass and taking water, the plow train proceeded to clear the west leg of the wye and the sidings there. This ended snow-removal operations for the first day. Locomotive 488 was cut out of the train, returning light to Chama. The OY, 487, and the rest of the train remained at Cumbres overnight.

At 7:30 a.m. on May 5, 488 departed Chama with the excursion train, which was scheduled to arrive at Cumbres by 8:45. From Cumbres, the excursion was to follow OY and 487 as far as Osier. Arrival at Osier was planned for 3:00 p.m.; the excursion train was to return to Chama by 6:00 that evening. Various events disrupted this schedule, however.

The first delay occurred when 488 stalled in the snow cuts below Windy Point. These cuts were in some of the drifts that had slowed OY so much on the previous day. Ice had formed on the rails overnight, causing 488 to lose adhesion. Eventually, 487 backed down from Cumbres to assist the 488 with its seven-car train to the top of the pass. After taking water, 488 and the excursion train followed the rotary train east as it cleared snow from Tanglefoot Curve.

A second delay came at a grade crossing near milepost 328, east of Cumbres. The flangeways of this crossing, covered by about three feet of snow, were filled with ice. OY had derailed on ice at this crossing in 1978, so, to clear the flangeways, the crossing was shoveled out by hand. Once the flangeways were opened, OY was able to plow the remainder of the drift.

These delays slowed the progress of the two trains so that Los Pinos tank, mile 325.25, was not reached until 4:00 p.m. At that point, the excursion train had to return to Chama. Rotary OY, with locomotive 487, continued east, plowing as far as Rock Tunnel. Thus ended an eventful two days of hard work by the C&TS crews. Several smaller drifts east of Osier were cleared by 487, equipped with its pilot plow, about a week later.

The snowplow train at Chama on the night of May 3, 1991. Equipment consisted of rotary OY, water car 0471, locomotives 487 and 488, two outfit cars, and caboose 0503. Photographs by William J. Lock, lighting by Richard Reiff.

The plow train departed Chama for Cumbres Pass a little after 10:00 on the morning of May 4, 1991. This view shows the train just north of the Rio Chama bridge.

BELOW, LEFT and RIGHT: At milepost 338, north of Dalton, New Mexico, 487 and 488 lift OY up the 4 percent grade. The first snow to be plowed was not encountered until the vicinity of Cresco tank, milepost 335. Photographs by Ernest W. Robart.

ABOVE: Working through a three-foot drift just below milepost 334, May 4, 1991.

Plowing into a small drift near mile 333.8, with the Wolf Creek valley as a backdrop. Although some snow had been encountered about half a mile below Cresco, sustained plowing did not begin for another half mile.

Rotary OY just above milepost 333, May 4, 1991. Photograph by James P. Bell, copyright 1991.

As plowing neared the Highway 17 grade crossing, between mileposts 333 and 332, clouds which had been gathering during the morning unleashed a series of snow squalls. These squalls, sometimes quite vigorous, characterized the weather for the remainder of the day. This photograph shows OY during one of the squalls as it nears the crossing, May 4, 1991.

Above the grade crossing, plowing — and the snow — continued. Photograph by Ernest W. Robart.

Rotary OY during a stop for lunch about half a mile below Coxo, Colorado, May 4, 1991.

Rotary OY pauses a short distance below milepost 331 to rebuild steam. Photograph by Ernest W. Robart.

After lunch, the plow train continued around Coxo loop to attack the deep drifts below Windy Point. This photograph shows the plow as it bites into a drift nearly fourteen feet deep on the uphill side. Photograph by Ernest W. Robart.

After clearing the deep drifts, the plow train, rounding Windy Point, works through snow about three feet deep, May 4, 1991. Photograph by Richard Sons.

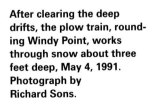

The plow train reached the summit of Cumbres Pass in mid-afternoon of May 4. This photograph shows OY as it advances past the standpipe and section house at Cumbres. Photograph by Ernest W. Robart.

As the snow squalls continue, OY works through another small drift between milepost 331 and the summit of Cumbres Pass, May 4, 1991. Photograph by Ernest W. Robart.

Before stopping for water, OY cleared the main track at Cumbres up to the highway crossing; the activity is observed by a portion of the crowd that had followed the train from Chama. Photograph by Ernest W. Robart.

After clearing the main track to the Highway 17 crossing, the train returned to the standpipe at Cumbres to take water. Then, the siding and west leg of the wye were plowed. In this view, OY is plowing the wye track, May 4, 1991.

Working through the Cumbres siding, east of the Highway 17 crossing, during one of the afternoon's snowy episodes.

On the morning of May 5, 1991, locomotive 488 pulled an excursion train out of Chama. This train, chartered by the Friends of the Cumbres & Toltec Scenic Railroad, was to follow the rotary train east from Cumbres. The 488 stalled on icy rails in the snow cuts below Windy Point, so 487 backed down to assist. Here, 487 arrives back at Cumbres with the excursion train. The plow train, followed by the excursion train, then proceeded east. Photograph by Ernest W. Robart.

East of Tanglefoot Curve at about mile 329.5. Photograph by Ernest W. Robart.

Rotary OY approaches milepost 330 at the west end of Tanglefoot Curve. The snow at this point was about three feet deep. Photograph by Ernest W. Robart.

Locomotive 488 with the Friends excursion train east of Tanglefoot Curve. Photograph by Ernest W. Robart.

As in 1978 and 1983, snow covered the Forest Service access road grade crossing at milepost 328. Flangeways in the crossing were filled with ice, so the crossing itself had to be shoveled out by hand. After the crossing and flangeways were cleared, OY plowed through the remainder of the drift, as shown in this photograph.

Rotary OY works through a drift just west of milepost 326. At the right of the photograph appear the remains of a snow fence, erected by the D&RGW in earlier years to alleviate drifting at this location.

The snowplow clears a small drift just east of the grade crossing, May 5, 1991.

The snow above milepost 326, about four feet deep, was plowed as a photo run-by for the excursionists; the rotary pilot, Earl Knoob, is keeping an eye on the photographers who are recording the event. Photograph by James P. Bell, copyright 1991.

By about 4:00 p.m. on May 5, the two trains had progressed as far east as Los Pinos tank. The excursion schedule constrained 488 to return its train to Chama, but 487 and OY continued east to Osier, clearing a large drift at that point. This view shows the plow train as it passes Los Pinos siding, on the opposite side of the loop from Los Pinos tank.

Track crossing Los Pinos valley was above the snow, but drifts along the mountain slopes required plowing. Although the railroad is on a south-facing slope, the grade acts as a bench; snow on the grade tends to be deeper and persist longer than snow on the slopes. In this photograph, as the train heads east down the Los Pinos valley, OY clears about two feet of snow from the track. After opening the track to Osier, the plow train returned to Chama, completing 1991's rotary snowplow operation. Photograph by Richard Sons.

Rotary snowplow OY working east from Cumbres Pass, approaching milepost 327, on the morning of May 6, 1993. The dense springtime snowpack was covered by about two inches of fresh snow which had fallen overnight.

OPENING THE RAILROAD
1993

Snow removal operations were again undertaken by the C&TS in the spring of 1993. Winter storms that broke a long-standing drought in California also brought heavy snow to the Rockies. Cumbres Pass received less snow than other parts of Colorado; still, in early April snow was about nine feet deep on the level at the summit. The snow was also more extensive than in earlier years, covering the track in places from below Cresco to within six miles of Antonito. Between Cresco and Cascade Creek, snow covered all but about three or four miles of the track. The big drift below Windy Point was over twenty feet high.

To cope with the situation, the C&TS anticipated using rotary OY for three days, May 3 through 5. Plowing as far east as the Whiplash, between Big Horn and Lava, was planned. On May 3, three locomotives were to push OY from Chama to Cumbres. On the second day, two locomotives and the rotary would open the track east of Cumbres, spending the night in Antonito. The third day was allowed for the return of the plow train to Chama. In actuality, four days of strenuous work were needed to open the railroad to Osier. The dense snowpack, generally about a foot deeper than in 1991, greatly slowed the rate at which the rotary could advance.

The plow train consisted of rotary OY; auxiliary water car 0471; locomotives 487, 497, and 488; a gondola of coal; three outfit cars; and caboose 0503. The train left Chama for Cumbres Pass as planned at 8:00 a.m. on May 3.

Some plowing was done between Lobato Trestle and the New Mexico Highway 17 grade crossing. A short, deep drift below Cresco was the first major obstacle, however. Between Cresco and Coxo, most of the track was covered by snow of two to three feet, with some deeper drifts. Progress was accordingly slow, the train reaching Coxo at about 3:45 p.m. At that point, it became clear that the train would not reach Cumbres before dark. Plowing ceased for the day so that the equipment could return to Chama before nightfall.

Each locomotive departed Coxo for Chama individually. The reverse moves were undertaken carefully, giving due regard to hazards inherent in backing the equipment over the newly-cleared track.

One of those hazards was encountered in a snow cut at milepost 336, below Cresco siding. Melt water seeping under the drift had softened the roadbed, causing the track to sink out of alignment. As 488 backed its portion of the train through the snow cut, wheels on the outfit cars tended to climb off the rails. Eventually, all of the cars behind the locomotive were eased over the soft track — but then 488's trailing wheels climbed off of the rails. After considerable work, the trailing truck was rerailed, and 488 took the outfit cars into Chama for the night.

No attempt was made to move the remainder of the plow train over the soft track. The track crew worked into the evening to make repairs; OY, 487, and 497 remained overnight at the west end of Cresco siding.

On May 4, the train crew returned to duty at 8:00 a.m. Considerable work was needed to service the locomotives, so plowing did not resume until early afternoon. The 488, which had spent the night in Chama, left town that morning fully replenished with water and coal. The two other locomotives had to take what water was available in the tank at Cresco — it was not sufficient to fill 497's tender. A front-end loader was used to add coal to the tenders of the OY, 487, and 497 at the Highway 17 crossing below Coxo. During the day, 497's water supply was replenished by shoveling snow into the tender tank.

Plowing resumed at Coxo at about 1:00 p.m. Although the snow was about five feet deep at Coxo, deeper drifts were still ahead. The formidable drift below Windy Point had been over twenty feet deep; the crest of this drift had been shoveled off by hand some days earlier to ease the task of plowing through it.

As in previous years, these deep drifts took several hours to clear. Gradual progress through the deep, dense snow was interrupted by pauses to rebuild the fire and restore steam pressure in OY's boiler. Finally, about 6:00 p.m., the train rounded Windy Point. Drifts several feet deep still blocked access to Cumbres, where a plentiful supply of water was available.

About one-eighth mile short of the summit, though, low water in the three locomotive tenders brought the train to a stop. While crew members shoveled snow into the tenders, fire trucks from Chama were called out to pump water up to the locomotives. Eventually, 487 and 497 held enough water to make steam. Plowing resumed, and the track to the standpipe was opened about 8:30 p.m. All equipment remained overnight at Cumbres.

After two days of hard work, activity on the morning of May 5 did not resume until 10:00. Again, servicing the equipment was the first task. The front-end loader was again employed to coal the tenders — a supply of coal had been dumped at the side of the highway the previous day. This work could only be done at the Cumbres highway crossing. The process was interrupted at intervals so that accumulated highway traffic could pass. As a result, plowing did not resume until about noon.

First, the wye and siding at Cumbres were plowed. After these tracks were opened, 488 left the outfit cars on the siding, turned on the wye, and headed back to Chama. Since east of Cumbres the train would be operating downhill, only two locomotives were required. The outfit cars were coupled to 497, and the rotary train proceeded east. Plowing continued until about 4:00 p.m., reaching milepost 327, about three and one-half miles to the east. The train then returned to Cumbres for the night.

On the morning of May 6, at Chama, 488

was readied to move ballast to the soft roadbed below Cresco. Pushing two cars of ballast, the locomotive departed Chama at about 8:00. Another car of ballast was taken up later in the day. A C&TS crew worked through the day to drain water and repair the track.

Plowing made steady progress on May 6. Osier, rather than Antonito, had become the goal. The C&TS had contracted to operate a special freight train on May 8. Allowing time to service the locomotives and otherwise prepare for the charter train meant that May 6 was the last day available for rotary operations. The track to Osier was cleared without incident by late afternoon on the 6th.

Warm weather during the following two weeks melted much of the snow that the plow train had not been able to reach. Still, as late as May 20, some snow lingered in cuts east of Osier. On that date, those remaining drifts were cleared by 487 with its pilot plow.

The 1993 trip illustrates the difficulties inherent in snow removal operations. Earl Knoob, pilot on the OY that year, commented,

"When the rotary was used in 1993, the poor thing was worked way beyond its design limits. In normal service, a rotary would be called out after a major storm, while the snow was still fresh and soft. The snow that we dealt with was extremely hard-packed, almost like pure ice. Every foot required the rotary to work very hard. Just as on a steam locomotive worked beyond its intended capacity, it became very difficult for the firemen to keep steam and water up in the boiler over long stretches: one injector could not keep the boiler full, and when the second injector was started, it was not possible to maintain steam pressure. So, periodically we had to stop to get steam and/or water up in the boiler. In 1983, I fired the OY and know how tough it is to keep trading water and steam all day. In 1983, there were stretches of snow that were not very deep, which allowed us to catch up on water and steam on occasion. The snows of 1993 were a lot tougher than when I fired. My hat is off to the guys who shoveled coal and nursed balky injectors for four days straight!"

Locomotives 487, 497, and 488 move rotary OY up the 4 percent grade near milepost 337 on the morning of May 3, 1993. The plow had already encountered small drifts of snow across the track, but the first deep drift was about three-quarters of a mile ahead of the train. Photograph by Ernest W. Robart.

Rotary OY encountered the first deep drifts just below milepost 336. In this view, below Cresco siding, the plow clears a drift about three feet deep. This location had less than a foot of snow in 1991; in 1983, it was clear. Photograph by Ernest W. Robart.

Plowing past Cresco siding, through snow about a foot deep, May 3, 1993. The siding, which is not generally used, was not opened. Photograph by Ernest W. Robart.

These two photographs, taken about a mile and a half above Cresco, show the plow train working through drifts ranging up to four feet deep. Photograph above by Ernest W. Robart.

ABOVE and RIGHT: Between milepost 333 and Coxo, snow averaged two to three feet in depth. These photographs show OY as it neared the Highway 17 grade crossing. Photograph above by Ernest W. Robart.

Rotary OY approaching Coxo, Colorado, May 3, 1993.

At a drift below Cresco (the same drift shown being plowed in the photograph at the left side of page 55), melt water, seeping under the snowpack, had softened the roadbed. The soft roadbed caused the track to subside out of alignment. Returning to Chama on the afternoon of May 3, 1993, 488 experienced considerable difficulty in moving its portion of the train over the weakened track. The cars were eventually eased over the trouble spot, but, when 488 attempted to back over the soft track, its trailing wheels climbed off the rails. The crew found it necessary to back the train through the cut before the trailing wheels could be rerailed. The 488 then continued to Chama with its portion of the train.

Though the C&TS track crew worked on the trouble spot into the evening, no attempt was made to move the rotary and two other locomotives over the weakened track. Instead, OY, 487, and 497 spent the night at the west end of Cresco siding. On the morning of May 4, the rotary and the two locomotives had to rely on the tank at Cresco for water; the supply was not adequate to fill 497's tender. Consequently, throughout the day crew members shoveled snow into 497's tender to keep the locomotive operating.

At the Highway 17 crossing below Coxo, a front-end loader was used to coal the tenders of OY, 487, and 497. The 488, which had spent the previous night in Chama, was serviced there before returning to the plow train.

Locomotive 488, its trailing truck off the rails, is stopped in the snow cut below Cresco on the afternoon of May 3, 1993.

About 3:45 in the afternoon of May 3, OY reached Coxo. Plowing was then suspended for the day because insufficient daylight remained to reach the summit of Cumbres Pass. Instead, the equipment was to be backed down to Chama for the night. Photograph by Ernest W. Robart.

ABOVE: Rotary snowplow OY at the west end of Cresco siding on the evening of May 3, 1993. Lighting by John Tully and Mike Del Vecchio.

Locomotives 487 and 497 move OY toward the Cresco water tank on the morning of May 4, 1993.

ABOVE: Coaling OY's tender at the Highway 17 crossing below Coxo, Colorado, about noon on May 4, 1993.

At Coxo, during a break in the plowing, 497's crew takes the opportunity to replenish the locomotive's water supply by shoveling snow into the tender tank.

LEFT and RIGHT: Plowing finally resumed at about 1:00 in the afternoon on May 4. Several deep drifts blocked the track between Coxo and Cumbres; these two photographs show OY attacking one of those drifts.
Photographs by
Ernest W. Robart.

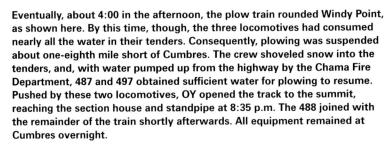

Eventually, about 4:00 in the afternoon, the plow train rounded Windy Point, as shown here. By this time, though, the three locomotives had consumed nearly all the water in their tenders. Consequently, plowing was suspended about one-eighth mile short of Cumbres. The crew shoveled snow into the tenders, and, with water pumped up from the highway by the Chama Fire Department, 487 and 497 obtained sufficient water for plowing to resume. Pushed by these two locomotives, OY opened the track to the summit, reaching the section house and standpipe at 8:35 p.m. The 488 joined with the remainder of the train shortly afterwards. All equipment remained at Cumbres overnight.

Rotary OY at Cumbres Pass on the morning of May 5, 1993. The weather, which had been partly cloudy the preceding day, left two inches of fresh snow during the night.

Track workers dig out switch points at Cumbres, May 5, 1993.

After servicing the equipment, it was necessary to plow the siding and west leg of the Cumbres wye (a bulldozer for which the C&TS had contracted had cleared the east leg of the wye several days earlier). This view shows the plow train at work clearing track east of the highway crossing, May 5, 1993.

After the wye and sidings were opened, 488 left its portion of the train (the gondola of coal, three outfit cars, and the caboose) on the siding at Cumbres, turned on the wye, and then headed back to Chama. East from Cumbres, the plowing was downhill so two locomotives were adequate for the work. In this photograph, 488 waits to depart Cumbres, as the weather becomes increasingly cloudy and windy.

Tanglefoot Curve, east of Cumbres Pass, for the most part is built on a low fill. As a result, the loop itself is usually kept free of snow by the wind. At the lower end of Tanglefoot, though, the track drops into the lee of the hill, opposite milepost 330. The OY, in these two views, works past the lower end of Tanglefoot Curve, May 5, 1993. The weather had turned to snow, driven by a brisk wind.
Photographs by
Ernest W. Robart.

LEFT and BELOW: Plowing between mileposts 329 and 328 on the afternoon of May 5, 1993.

Rotary OY at the grade crossing near milepost 328. A photograph taken at this location in 1983 appears on page 37. The track was cleared for about three-quarters of a mile beyond this crossing before plowing ceased for the day. The train then backed to Cumbres for the night.

Schedule commitments dictated that May 6, 1993, was the last day available for snow-plow operations. The track from near milepost 327 to Osier, about 8.6 miles to the east, remained to be cleared. Once again, at Cumbres, the front-end loader was called upon to replenish the coal supply in the tenders. After taking coal and water, the train returned to milepost 327, where plowing resumed about noon. The downhill direction of the train, plus an absence of the excessively deep drifts which had delayed progress on the west side of Cumbres Pass, facilitated the work. Still, the average speed of the train was about four miles per hour.

Rotary OY plowing up to Los Pinos tank, mile 325.3, at about 1:30 in the afternoon, May 6, 1993.

Coaling OY's tender at Cumbres, Colorado, in the face of a brisk wind and blowing snow on the morning of May 6, 1993.

The plow train just above milepost 326, May 6, 1993.

ABOVE: Los Pinos loop, built, as is Tanglefoot Curve, on a low fill above the floor of the valley, was mostly clear of snow. On the east side of the valley, though, along the flanks of the mountains, snow two to five feet deep was encountered. This photograph shows the rotary train at work along the east side of the Los Pinos valley, between mileposts 324 and 323. Most of the track between this point and Cascade Creek was covered by varying amounts of snow. The OY reached Osier at about 5:00 p.m. on May 6.

ABOVE: Although the rotary train was not able to reach drifts east of Osier, much of that snow melted in the following two weeks. A few drifts remained in cuts, however. Locomotive 487, with its pilot plow, was dispatched to plow these drifts on May 20, 1993. In this photograph, 487 pauses while breaking loose the snow in a cut at milepost 317 on May 20. This view shows how resistant the dense snow can be to plowing. Photograph by Earl G. Knoob.

LEFT: Rotary OY pauses after clearing the last drift at Osier, Colorado, late in the afternoon of May 6, 1993. Following this photograph, the equipment was moved back to Chama, completing four days of arduous work. Photograph by Earl G. Knoob.

Cool weather during the spring of 1994 delayed the thaw on Cumbres Pass, prompting the Cumbres & Toltec to operate rotary OY from Chama to Osier. The operation was completed in one day, May 18, 1994. Nearly all of the snow to be removed was between the Highway 17 grade crossing below Coxo and milepost 329, east of Tanglefoot Curve. In this view, OY is shown plowing a five-foot drift just below Windy Point at about noon on the 18th.

OPENING THE RAILROAD
1994

Precipitation during the winter of 1993–1994 was not exceptional; there was no anticipation that, with the arrival of spring, warmer weather would not melt the snowpack on Cumbres in time for passenger excursions to begin on schedule. Spring, though, brought cool weather and more snow. The spring storms did not add to the depth of snow at Cumbres so much as they retarded the melting of the deeper drifts, particularly those just below Windy Point. By late April 1994, some drifts were still over eight feet deep. With less than a month before passenger trains were to run, the Cumbres & Toltec track crew still had not been able to inspect fully the 64-mile line.

As time passed, it became clear that the drifts would have to be removed mechanically; the location of the drifts and the extent of snow over other portions of the railroad shaded by terrain or vegetation made it impractical to clear the track with bulldozers. Early in May, C&TS no. 19, a diesel-electric switch engine at Antonito, ran west from that point to plow snow from some of the cuts between Sublette and Osier. As the cool weather persisted, it became clear that rotary OY once again would be needed to clear the deeper drifts which still covered the track over Cumbres Pass. Monday, May 16, was tentatively fixed as the date of the rotary operation, and OY was moved into the shop at Chama for inspection and servicing.

Melting snow once again had softened the roadbed near milepost 336 below Cresco, where melt water had caused so much trouble the year before. Additional work on the track was required before the heavy snow-plow train could move over it. Several cars of ballast were moved to the soft track on the 16th, delaying the rotary train for two days.

Pushed by locomotives 489 and 484, OY and auxiliary water car 0471 departed Chama about 8:50 on the morning of May 18. Behind 484 were a gondola of coal, an outfit car, and caboose 05635. Although the train crew expected to finish work the same day, the carload of coal was included so that fuel would be available should plowing be delayed by some unforeseen circumstance.

Progress, though, was much as anticipated. The track below Cresco caused no difficulty, although a broken air hose at that point delayed the train for about three-quarters of an hour. The first continuous snow was encountered above the Highway 17 grade crossing below Coxo. Even there, the depth was not more than a foot in most places. The only difficult plowing took place, as expected, just below Windy Point. There, one drift five feet deep took about fifteen minutes to clear. The plow train reached Windy Point about 12:17 in the afternoon.

Next to the Cumbres section house was another drift about four feet deep. This drift was cleared, and the main track was opened east of the Cumbres highway crossing by about 12:55. After a stop for water and lunch, work resumed to clear the siding and west leg of the wye at Cumbres. The last significant snow to be plowed covered the siding and main track east of Highway 17 for a distance of about half a mile. The depth did not exceed three feet.

On Tanglefoot Curve and beyond, only isolated drifts

C&TS rotary OY in the yard at Chama, New Mexico, April 27, 1994. Late spring storms such as this one, which left about three inches of snow on the ground by the following morning, delayed the spring thaw at higher elevations. Three weeks after this photograph, OY was operated east to Osier, clearing snow up to five feet deep from the railroad.

were encountered. A track car from Antonito had traveled west as far as Osier earlier that day, verifying that the line was clear between those two points. To ensure that the railroad between Los Pinos and Osier was free of snow, the plow train proceeded east. It reached Osier about 3:30 in the afternoon.

At Osier a balloon loop had been installed the year before to turn passenger trains. All the equipment except OY was turned on the loop before making the trip back to Chama. The rotary was pulled back to Chama; by turning the locomotives on the loop, the train crew avoided the awkward move of backing the equipment to the wye at Cumbres. OY was back in Chama with its fire dropped before sunset, ending the C&TS's briefest rotary operation in over a decade.

ABOVE: Rotary OY and its train about a mile above Cresco, May 18, 1994. Snow at this location in 1993 had been about four feet deep.

BELOW: West of the Highway 17 grade crossing below Coxo more extensive patches of snow covered the track. Rotary OY is shown here working through snow about a foot deep.

Near mile 332.8, OY passes through a small drift — just enough snow to rotate the wheel.

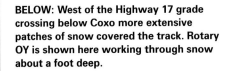

ABOVE: The scene at Chama on the evening of May 17, 1994, the day before the rotary operation. Rotary OY and behind it locomotive 489 have been readied for the trip and are under steam. The second locomotive used, 484, is out of view in the shop building behind 489. To the left of the rotary is locomotive 487, its boiler jacket and other parts removed as part of a boiler inspection. On the track to OY's right, locomotives 488 and 497 are under steam for preseason tests. At the far right, on the engine house lead, K-27 locomotive 463 is also under steam. Last operated by the Rio Grande in the early 1950s, 463 was overhauled by the C&TS during 1993–1994 and returned to service. Its first test run out of Chama, to Lobato, took place two days after this photograph. Thus, for the first time in about thirty years, there were six live boilers in Chama — giving the engine watchman plenty of work over the night.

TOP LEFT: The deepest drifts, those which necessitated the rotary operation, were in their usual location, just below Windy Point. In all, OY took nearly half an hour to plow drifts ranging up to about five feet deep. Photograph by Ernest W. Robart.

BOTTOM LEFT: Rotary OY after exiting the last drift on Windy Point.

TOP RIGHT: The last snow of any depth encountered was a drift about four feet deep, formed in the lee of the Cumbres section house. Rotary OY is shown here plowing past the section house and standpipe about 12:30 p.m., May 18, 1994.

BOTTOM RIGHT: The rotary throwing about two feet of heavy, wet snow off of the main track at Cumbres Pass. Photograph by Ernest W. Robart.

Clearing a small drift at the east end of Tanglefoot Curve, opposite milepost 330. Photographs on page 62 show the snowplow working at approximately the same location the previous year. Photograph by Ernest W. Robart.

Between Tanglefoot Curve and milepost 329, drifted snow up to about eighteen inches deep still covered the track in places. The rotary in this photograph is working through one of those small drifts near mile 329.5.

TOP and BOTTOM RIGHT: Near Los Pinos tank, more small drifts were encountered, mostly in cuts or areas shaded by trees. In these two views, OY is at work in the vicinity of milepost 326, about half a mile west of the water tank.

After clearing snow from the track along the east side of the Los Pinos valley, east of Los Pinos tank, the plow train continued as far as Osier. A balloon loop installed during the summer of 1993 permitted the equipment to be turned for the trip back to Chama. In this photograph, the train has been divided into two sections. Locomotive 484 with the gondola of coal, the outfit car, and caboose is shown here ready to depart for Chama. The cut at milepost 318, less than half a mile east of Osier, in past years contained a snow drift which was opened using the rotary plow. No plowing was required this far east in 1994. Above and behind 484 can be seen 489 with the remainder of the train. Photograph by Ernest W. Robart.

About 4:00 p.m., ten minutes after 484's departure, 489 leads rotary OY and its water car past the west switch of the balloon loop, on the return trip to Chama. Photograph by Ernest W. Robart.

C&TS rotary OY in Chama on the morning of May 19, 1994. A little snow remains as evidence of the previous day's work. Below the second window to the left of the pilot house door can be seen several new boards — the paint is a little darker and is peeling from a couple of the boards. This new siding was added during a 1993 Friends of the C&TS volunteer work session. It replaced boards which vibrated off of the rotary's carbody during the strenuous rotary expedition of May 3–6, 1993.

Windy Point Press and the
Friends of the Cumbres & Toltec Scenic Railroad

The Windy Point Press is the publishing arm of the Friends of the Cumbres & Toltec Scenic Railroad, Inc. The Friends is dedicated to the preservation and interpretation of the Cumbres & Toltec Scenic Railroad. We work closely with the Cumbres & Toltec Scenic Railroad Commission (of the states of Colorado and New Mexico), which owns the railroad, and Kyle Railways, which operates the railroad.

The Friends of the Cumbres & Toltec Scenic Railroad, Inc., has had a major impact on the restoration, reconstruction, and preservation of historic equipment and buildings along the railroad line. During the 1980s, our efforts were primarily designed to stabilize, paint, and letter all of the existing rolling stock, which is the most extensive collection of narrow gauge equipment extant. In 1990, our focus broadened to also include the stabilization and restoration of the buildings and sites of historic interest along the line.

The mission of the Friends also includes preserving records, relics, and other items of historic interest, as well as promoting public knowledge of and interest in local and national history, particularly as it relates to the Cumbres & Toltec Scenic Railroad and its predecessor, the Denver & Rio Grande Western Railroad.

From its incorporation in 1988, the Friends has grown to more than one thousand members around the world. Members receive a quarterly newsletter describing in detail the current events and history of the C&TS. They also have the opportunity to become volunteers and work on the property during work sessions held primarily during the summer months. Finally, members receive discounts on regular train rides as well as special charter rides and are kept up to date about historical publications and other merchandise of interest.

Some of the major projects which the Friends has undertaken and completed prior to 1994 include the following:

- The return of six original tank cars to the C&TS from Alaska.
- The completion of a dual-gauge display track in Antonito, Colorado, complete with standard gauge idler car and two standard gauge box cars.
- The return of six original double-deck sheep cars to the C&TS.
- The purchase of two historic passenger cars.
- The complete restoration of the remaining seven bays of the Cumbres snowshed.
- The exterior restoration of section houses and log cabins along the 64-mile line.
- The restoration of dozens of freight cars ranging from repainting cars to totally rebuilding maintenance-of-way equipment.
- The surveying and documentation of cars and buildings for future work as well as historic preservation.

Profits from the sale of this book will be used for historic preservation purposes.

Friends of the C&TS
P.O. Box 222
Chama, NM 87520